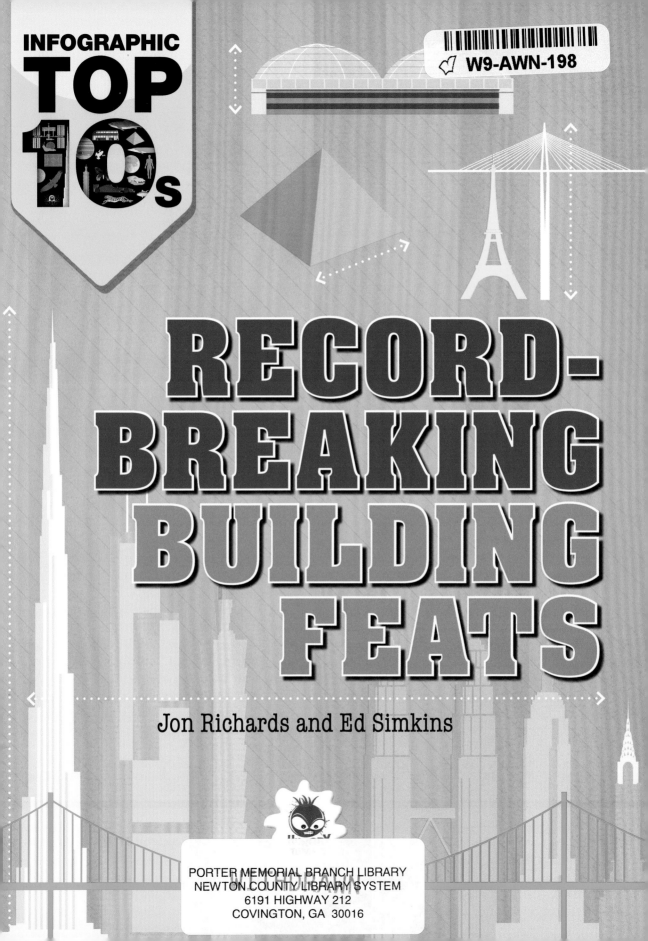

INFOGRAPHIC TOP 10s

RECORD-BREAKING BUILDING FEATS

Jon Richards and Ed Simkins

CONTENTS

‹ ·············· ›

4 **Taller and Taller**

6 Spend, Spend, Spend

8 **No Expense Spared**

10 On Display

12 **Fun and Games**

14 Building for Animals

16 **Fit for a King**

18 Ancient Buildings

20 **On the Move**

22 Bridging the Gap

24 **That Doesn't Look Right!**

26 Superdomes

28 **Building in Space**

30 Glossary

31 Websites

32 Index

pages 4-5
See which buildings have held the record for being the world's tallest over the last 100 years.

WELCOME!

<‹ ························· ›>

From the tallest to the longest and from the busiest to the largest, this book looks at fantastic record-breaking buildings from all over the planet and beyond! It uses stunning icons, graphics, and visualizations to show you how these structures have raised the bar in the construction industry.

pages 28-29
Find out just how big a space station can be and what's inside.

pages 12-13
Discover how fast the world's quickest roller coasters can travel.

pages 18-19
Read about how ancient peoples built some of the greatest monuments on the planet.

pages 16-17
Learn about the staggering size of the world's biggest palaces.

TALLER AND TALLER

Advances in technology over the last 100 years have seen the world's tallest buildings nearly quadruple in size. The biggest modern skyscrapers are more than half a mile (0.8 kilometers) high and really do have their heads in the clouds!

Moving Tower

Changes in temperature throughout the year cause the Eiffel Tower to expand and contract by as much as 7.1 inches (18 centimeters). Powerful winds also push the top of the tower, causing it to sway by 2.8 inches (7 cm).

2.8 inches (7 cm)

At just 988 feet (301 meters) tall, the Eiffel Tower in Paris is less than half the height of the Burj Khalifa.

These graphics show

the buildings that have held the title of the world's tallest building over the last 100 years. They are compared to the height of a giraffe.

1

2

3

4

5

6

7

8

9

10

× 74

× 70

4

TALLEST BUILDINGS THROUGH HISTORY

1. Burj Khalifa, Dubai (since 2010)—2,717 feet (828 m)

2. Taipei 101, Taiwan (2004–2007)—1,670 feet (509 m)

3. Petronas Towers, Malaysia (1998–2004)—1,483 feet (452 m)

4. Willis Tower, United States (1974–1998)—1,450 feet (442 m)

5. World Trade Center, United States (1972–1974)—1,368 feet (417 m)

6. Empire State Building, United States (1931–1972)—1,250 feet (381 m)

7. Chrysler Building, United States (1930–1931)—1,047 feet (319 m)

8. The Trump Tower, United States (1930)—928 feet (283 m)

9. Woolworth Building, United States (1913–1930)—791 feet (241 m)

10. Metropolitan Life Building, United States (1909–1913)—699 feet (213 m)

× 36   × 40   × 47   × 53   × 64   × 75   × 85   × 138

Empire State Building

Lightning strikes this skyscraper an average of 23 times a year.

The observatory on the 102nd floor was originally designed to be a check-in area for airships that would moor to the top.

5

SPEND, SPEND, SPEND

Shopping malls are enormous buildings that can contain hundreds of stores. Many of the largest malls also feature theme parks, restaurants, and movie theaters to keep shoppers happy and spending money.

Mega mall

The Dubai Mall is the largest mall in the world in total area, but only the 14th largest in leasable area (the area taken up by stores).

shops 1,200

200 restaurants

It has the world's largest candy store—Candylicious. This covers 10,010 square feet (930 sq. m), which is about **1.5 soccer fields**.

It has 80 million visitors every year...

Germany: population 80,996,000

...more than any other place on Earth and close to the total population of Germany.

Total area = 12,099,000 square feet (1,124,000 sq. m)

Leasable area = 3,770,000 square feet (350,000 sq. m)

Vatican City 4,740,000 square feet (440,000 sq. m)

Supermarkets

The first supermarket in the United States was King Kullen Supermarket, which opened on Jamaica Avenue, New York City, in August 1930.

It covered just 6,028 square feet (560 sq. m) —a basketball court is about 4,520 square feet (420 sq. m).

In contrast, Jungle Jim's International Market in Ohio covers more than 199,100 square feet (18,500 sq. m)—more than 30 times the area of King Kullen Supermarket and three times the area of the White House.

Walmart is one of the biggest supermarket chains in the world.

It has...

more than 11,000 stores in **27 countries** and employs **2.2 million people.**

LARGEST SHOPPING MALLS (LEASABLE AREA)

1. **New South China Mall (Dongguan, China)—6,459,993 square feet (600,153 sq. m)**

2. Golden Resources Mall (Beijing, China)—6,000,008 square feet (557,419 sq. m)

3. **SM Megamall (Mandaluyong, Philippines)—5,451,221 square feet (506,435 sq. m)**

4. SM City North EDSA (Quezon City, Philippines)—5,197,656 square feet (482,878 sq. m)

5. **1 Utama (Petaling Jaya, Selangor, Malaysia)—5,005,218 square feet (465,000 sq. m)**

6. Persian Gulf Complex (Shiraz, Iran)—4,843,760 square feet (450,000 sq. m)

7. **Central World (Bangkok, Thailand)—4,623,100 square feet (429,500 sq. m)**

8. Isfahan City Center (Isfahan, Iran)—4,574,662 square feet (425,000 sq. m)

9. **Mid Valley Megamall (Kuala Lumpur, Malaysia)—4,520,842 square feet (420,000 sq. m)**

=9. Cevahir Mall (Istanbul, Turkey)—4,520,842 square feet (420,000 sq. m)

NO EXPENSE SPARED

Welcome to the most expensive buildings on the planet! They offer special office services, amazing hotel accommodations, and the height of private luxury.

1 **2** **3** **4** **5** **6** **7** **8** **9** **10**

Linking the hotel's three towers is an enormous skypark, which is big enough for 4.5 Airbus A380s to fit on.

Marina Bay Sands

The hotel also features a swimming pool that is **492 feet (150 m) long**, a shopping mall, a museum, two theaters, and an ice rink.

It was built at a rate of one floor **every four days**.

The largest suites in the Marina Bay Sands measure 6,771 square feet (629 sq. m), about the same area as **two tennis courts**.

The casino inside the hotel has a chandelier that contains 132,000 crystals and weighs 7.8 tons (7.1 metric tons)—about the weight of three adult hippos!

MOST EXPENSIVE BUILDINGS

1. **Marina Bay Sands (Singapore)—$6 billion**
2. Resorts World Sentosa (Singapore)—$5.38 billion
3. **Emirates Palace (Abu Dhabi)—$4.46 billion**
4. The Cosmopolitan (United States)—$4.16 billion
5. **The Shard (United Kingdom)—$3.9 billion**
6. One World Trade Center (United States)—$3.8 billion
7. **Wynn Resort (United States)—$3.26 billion**
8. Venetian Macao (Macau)—$2.97 billion
9. **City of Dreams (Macau)—$2.75 billion**
10. Antilia (India)—$2.53 billion

The prices of these buildings have been adjusted for inflation so that the figures here show the cost if they were all built in 2012.

Living in luxury

The Burj al Arab is a seven-star hotel in Dubai. It has nine restaurants and bars, a health spa, four swimming pools, its own private beach, and a helicopter landing pad on the roof.

×9   ×4   ×1   ×1

Most expensive hotel suite

The Royal Penthouse Suite at the Hotel President Wilson in Geneva, Switzerland, can cost up to **$83,200 a night**.

It has 12 bedrooms, 12 bathrooms, a gym, a pool table, and a grand piano.

The suite covers 19,375 square feet (1,800 sq. m)—larger than the area of four basketball courts.

Antilia

Antilia is said to be the most expensive private residence in the world. It has **three helipads** and a multistory garage with space for **168 cars**.

168

...... Owned by Indian billionaire Mukesh Ambani, Antilia is located in the city of **Mumbai, India**.

558 feet (170 m)

305 feet (93 m)

ON DISPLAY

Millions of people flock to museums around the world every year. These buildings house precious works of art, animal bones and fossils, historical relics and monuments, or amazing inventions. They also have huge storage areas where they keep objects that they cannot display.

1
2
3
4

= 500,000 visitors

The Smithsonian

The Smithsonian Institution is the world's largest museum complex. It is made up of 19 galleries and museums and houses more than

137 million objects.

If you spent one minute looking at each object for 24 hours a day, it would take more than 260 years to view them all!

1 min. × × 24 hrs.

= 260 years

The British Museum

It has a total area of 990,280 square feet (92,000 sq. m), of which 232,500 square feet (21,600 sq. m) is storage space (with a further 101,181 square feet (9,400 sq. m) of storage space off-site).

The British Museum can display about 80,000 items at any one time— but that's just 1 percent of the 8 million items it owns.

MOST POPULAR MUSEUMS

1. **Louvre (Paris)—9,334,000 visitors a year**

2. **National Museum of Natural History (Washington, DC)—8,000,000**

3. **National Museum of China (Beijing)—7,450,000**

4. **National Air and Space Museum (Washington, DC)—6,970,000**

5. **British Museum (London)—6,701,000**

6. **The Metropolitan Museum of Art (New York City)—6,280,000**

7. **National Gallery (London)—6,031,000**

8. **Vatican Museums (Vatican)—5,459,000**

9. **Natural History Museum (London)—5,250,000**

10. **American Museum of Natural History (New York City)—5,000,000**

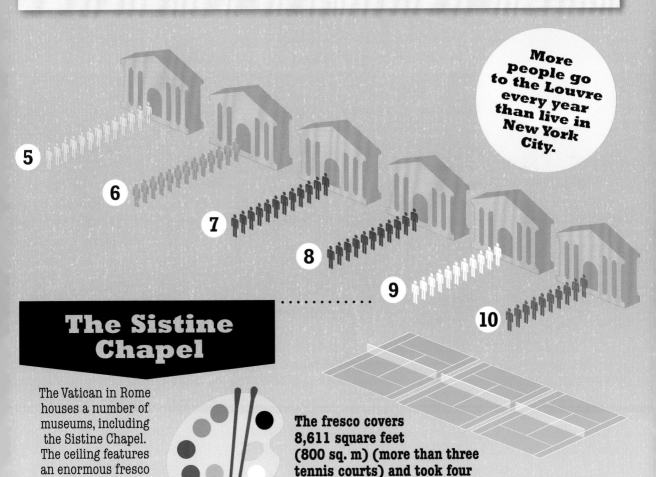

More people go to the Louvre every year than live in New York City.

The Sistine Chapel

The Vatican in Rome houses a number of museums, including the Sistine Chapel. The ceiling features an enormous fresco painted by Michelangelo.

The fresco covers 8,611 square feet (800 sq. m) (more than three tennis courts) and took four years to paint (1508–1512).

FUN AND GAMES

Strap in, hold on, and get ready to discover the adrenalin-fueled world of the planet's top theme parks! They cater to millions of people and offer the most thrilling rides on Earth.

3 Top Thrill Dragster
Cedar Point, Sandusky, Ohio
119 miles (192 km) per hour

4 Dodonpa
Fuji-Q Highland, Yamanashi, Japan
106.4 miles (171.2 km) per hour

=5 Tower of Terror
Dreamworld, Queensland, Australia
99.4 miles (160 km) per hour

=5 Superman: Escape from Krypton
Six Flags Magic Mountain, Valencia, California
99.4 miles (160 km) per hour

Tallest roller coaster

The tallest roller coaster in the world is the Tower of Terror at Dreamworld amusement park in Queensland, Australia. It is 377.33 feet (115 m) tall—more than twice the height of **Nelson's Column**, London, at 171 feet (52 m), and a little shorter than **St. Peter's Basilica**, Rome, which is 453 feet (138 m) tall.

10 Leviathan
Canada's Wonderland, Ontario, Canada
91.5 miles (147.2 km) per hour

2 Kingda Ka
Six Flags Great Adventure, Jackson, New Jersey
127.3 miles (204.8 km) per hour

1 Formula Rossa
Ferrari World, Yas Island, Abu Dhabi
148.3 miles (238.6 km) per hour

Ferrari World is the largest indoor amusement park in the world. It covers a total of 2,153,000 square feet (200,000 sq. m), and the indoor area is 926,000 square feet (86,000 sq. m)—as big as seven football fields.

Ferrari World

Formula Rossa at Ferrari World in Abu Dhabi is the fastest roller coaster in the world. It accelerates from **0 to 62 miles (100 km) per hour in 2 seconds**—that's as fast as a Formula 1 car.

7 Ring Racer
Nürburgring, Nürburg, Germany
98.7 miles (159 km) per hour

8 Steel Dragon
Nagashima Spa Land, Nagashima, Japan
94 miles (152 km) per hour

9 Millennium Force
Cedar Point, Sandusky, Ohio
92.5 miles (148.8 km) per hour

In total, the 10 most popular theme parks attract 126,669,000 people every year—that's more than the total population of Mexico.

BUILDING FOR ANIMALS

Animals need lots of space to live in—some zoos cover enormous areas! Aquariums also need to meet each animal's specific needs and be supertough to withstand tons of water and strong beasts.

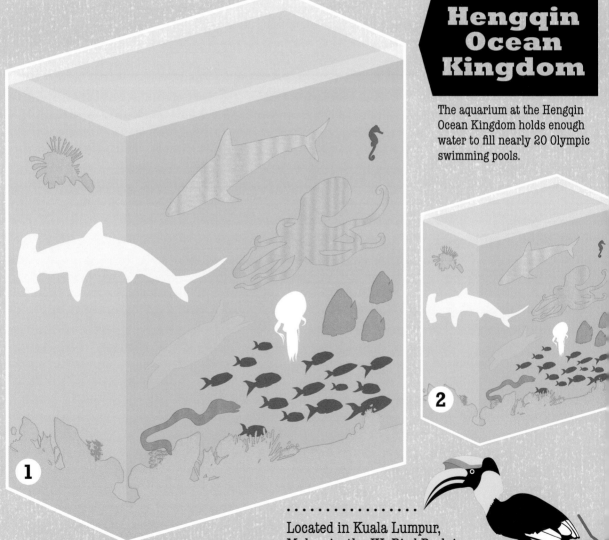

1

2

Big bird park

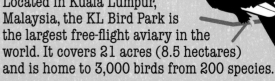

Located in Kuala Lumpur, Malaysia, the KL Bird Park is the largest free-flight aviary in the world. It covers 21 acres (8.5 hectares) and is home to 3,000 birds from 200 species.

LARGEST AQUARIUMS

1. **Hengqin Ocean Kingdom (China)—12.87 million gallons (48.72 million liters)**

2. Georgia Aquarium (United States)—6.3 million gallons (23.84 million liters)

3. **Dubai Mall Aquarium (Dubai)—2.64 million gallons (9.99 million liters)**

4. Okinawa Churaumi Aquarium (Japan)—2 million gallons (7.5 million liters)

5. **Oceanogràfic (Spain)—1.8 million gallons (7 million liters)**

6. Turkuazoo (Turkey)—1.3 million gallons (5 million liters)

7. **Monterey Bay Aquarium (United States)—1.2 million gallons (4.54 million liters)**

8. uShaka Marine World (South Africa)—<1 million gallons (3.8 million liters)

=8. **Shanghai Ocean Aquarium (China)—<1 million gallons (3.8 million liters)**

=8. Aquarium of Genoa (Italy)—<1 million gallons (3.8 million liters)

The penguin pool at London Zoo covers 13,000 square feet (1,200 sq. m) and holds 119,000 gallons (450,000 liters). That's enough to fill more than 5,500 bathtubs and give you a bath every day for the next 15 years!

× 5,500

Penguin pool

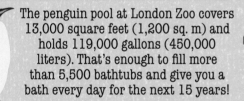

One wall of the Dubai Mall Aquarium is made from an enormous panel of transparent acrylic—the largest in the world. It measures 107.87 feet (32.88 m) by 27.2 feet (8.3 m), making it bigger than a tennis court.

Toronto Zoo

Toronto Zoo is one of the largest zoos in the world. It has more than 5,000 animals from 500 different species.

The zoo has 6 miles (10 km) of walking trails (enough to go around an athletics track 25 times) and covers 709 acres (287 hectares)—about the same size as Central Park in Manhattan.

- - - Central Park

Manhattan

FIT FOR A KING

Royal palaces are some of the most opulent and imposing buildings on the planet. Inside, the rooms are decked out in the height of luxury.

The Hall of Mirrors at the Palace of Versailles in France contains **357** mirrors.

The enormous Louvre palace in Paris covers more than 1.5 times the area of the Pentagon.

The Forbidden City

The Forbidden City in Beijing is part of a huge palace complex that covers **183 acres** (74 hectares) in total.

That's three times the area of the Capitol Building in Washington, DC.

Palace of Parliament, Bucharest

It is the world's heaviest building, with **770,000 tons** (700,000 metric tons) of steel and bronze...

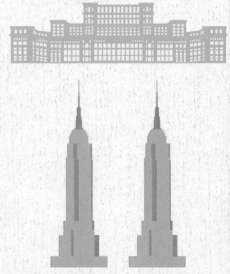

...that's twice the weight of the Empire State Building.

LARGEST ROYAL PALACES

1. **Louvre (Paris, France)**—2,260,000 square feet (210,000 sq. m)

2. Istana Nurul Iman (Bandar Seri Begawan, Brunei)—2,150,000 square feet (200,000 sq. m)

3. **Apostolic Palace (Vatican City)**—1,744,000 square feet (162,000 sq. m)

4. Forbidden City (Beijing, China)—1,615,000 square feet (150,000 sq. m)

5. **Royal Palace of Madrid (Madrid, Spain)**—1,453,000 square feet (135,000 sq. m)

6. Quirinal Palace (Rome, Italy)—1,189,400 square feet (110,500 sq. m)

7. **Buckingham Palace (London, United Kingdom)**—829,000 square feet (77,000 sq. m)

8. Topkapi Palace (Istanbul, Turkey)—750,000 square feet (70,000 sq. m)

9. **Palace of Versailles (Versailles, France)**—721,000 square feet (67,000 sq. m)

10. Royal Palace of Stockholm (Stockholm, Sweden)—657,890 square feet (61,120 sq. m)

It has 35 million cubic feet (1 million cu. m) of marble

—that's enough to fill

400
Olympic swimming pools.

Inside, there are **3,858 tons** (3,500 metric tons) of glass, which is equivalent to the weight of…

…17.5 blue whales.

The glass is used in **1,409** lights and mirrors, and…

…**480** chandeliers.

It has

2,200,000 square feet (200,000 sq. m) of carpet

—enough to cover…

…**4 polo fields.**

ANCIENT BUILDINGS

The oldest surviving buildings in the world were built nearly 7,000 years ago. These ancient constructions are usually tombs, monuments or, like Stonehenge, puzzling structures whose real use remains a mystery.

Stonehenge

This ancient monument was started about **5,000 years** ago and built over a period of **1,000 years**.

Each stone weighs 24.8 tons (22.5 metric tons)…

…as much as four elephants.

How it was built

Larger stones were levered into pits until they stood upright. Smaller stones were then raised using levers and platforms, before being pushed into place on top of the upright stones.

stone
lever
rollers
ropes
pit
logs

The larger stones were moved on rollers into place by a pit. One end of the stone was then raised using a lever.

Logs were placed under the raised end to keep it in place. The lever was used again to raise the stone even higher.

Ropes were then attached to lift the stone so that it was upright, with one end in the pit.

Finally, the pit was filled in, to hold the upright stone firmly in place.

OLDEST BUILDINGS IN THE WORLD

1. **Barnenez, France—around 4800 BCE**

=1. Tumulus of Bougon, France—around 4800 BCE

=1. **Tumulus Saint-Michel, France—around 4800 BCE**

4. Wayland's Smithy, United Kingdom—around 3700 BCE

=4. **Knap of Howar, United Kingdom—around 3700 BCE**

=4. Ggantija, Malta—around 3700 BCE

7. **West Kennet Long Barrow, United Kingdom—around 3650 BCE**

8. Listoghil, Ireland—around 3550 BCE

9. **Sechin Bajo, Peru—around 3500 BCE**

=9. La Hougue Bie, Jersey—around 3500 BCE

Great pyramids

Egypt has about **140 pyramids**, which were built as burial chambers for important people. They can be stepped; bent; or have a true, triangular shape.

These ancient buildings were constructed more than 4,500 years ago. The **Great Pyramid of Khufu** is the largest and it contains **2.3 million stones**, and weighs more than **5.5 million tons** (5 million metric tons).

It was originally 482 feet (147 m) tall and was the tallest building in the world for more than 3,500 years.

The heavy stones were dragged by teams of workers up ramps that wrapped around the pyramid.

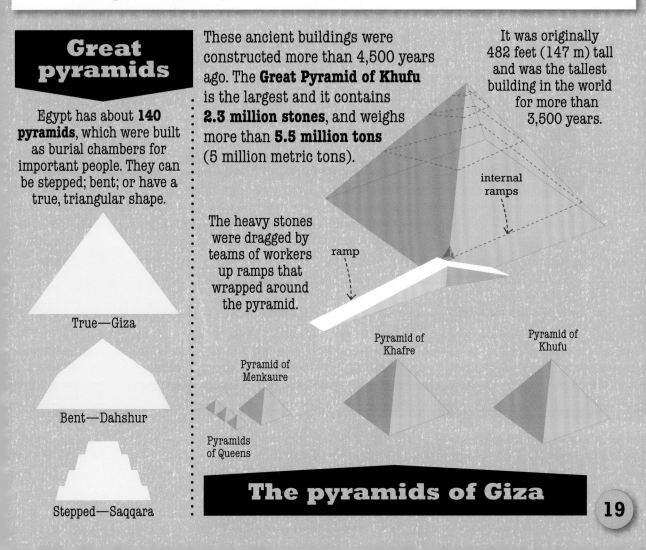

True—Giza

Bent—Dahshur

Stepped—Saqqara

internal ramps

ramp

Pyramid of Menkaure

Pyramids of Queens

Pyramid of Khafre

Pyramid of Khufu

The pyramids of Giza

ON THE MOVE

Millions of people travel around the globe every year, flying from huge airports or boarding trains from busy stations. At the same time, enormous cargo ships carry billions of tons of cargo to bustling ports and freight terminals.

= 5,000,000 passengers

1

2

3

4

5

Busiest port

The world's busiest port is Shanghai, China, which handles **32.53 million TEUs** of cargo every single year.

6

BUSIEST AIRPORTS

1. **Atlanta—94,778,483 passengers per year**

2. Beijing, China—84,187,266

3. **Heathrow, United Kingdom—73,036,493**

4. Tokyo, Japan—70,680,743

5. **Los Angeles—68,783,018**

6. Dubai, United Arab Emirates (UAE)—68,445,520

7. **Chicago (O'Hare)—68,329,963**

8. Paris (Charles de Gaulle Airport), France—63,311,851

9. **Dallas/Fort Worth—61,744,158**

10. Hong Kong, China—61,485,440

About 93 percent of the passengers traveling through Heathrow Airport are using international flights. That figure for Atlanta airport is around 10 percent.

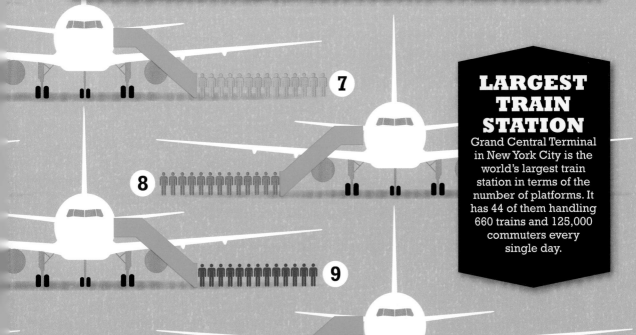

LARGEST TRAIN STATION

Grand Central Terminal in New York City is the world's largest train station in terms of the number of platforms. It has 44 of them handling 660 trains and 125,000 commuters every single day.

TEU stands for "twenty-foot equivalent units," which is the size of a standard shipping container. One of these holds **1,360 cubic feet** (38.5 cu. m), which is about...

...250 full baths of water.

This means that Shanghai handles about **44 billion cubic feet** (1.25 billion cu. m) of cargo every year, or **4,900,000 cubic feet** (140,000 cu. m) every single hour (working 24 hours a day and 365 days a year!).

That's enough to fill 20 blimps.

BRIDGING THE GAP

The world's greatest bridges are amazing feats of technology. They are capable of carrying thousands of tons of trucks, cars, and buses over wide rivers, deep valleys, and even whole stretches of ocean.

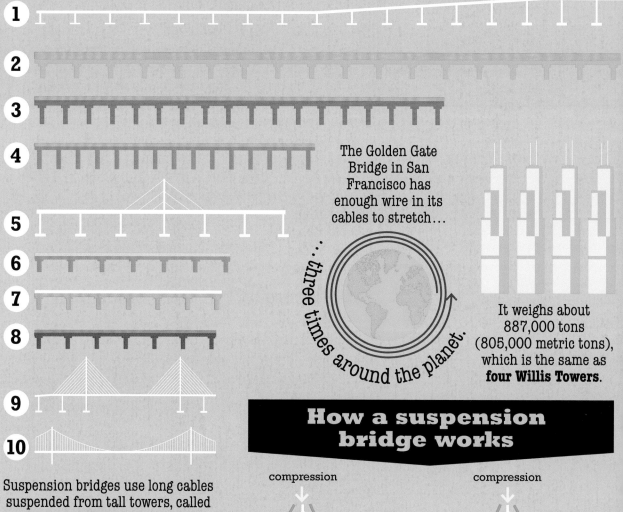

1

2

3

4

5

6

7

8

9

10

The Golden Gate Bridge in San Francisco has enough wire in its cables to stretch...

...three times around the planet.

It weighs about 887,000 tons (805,000 metric tons), which is the same as **four Willis Towers**.

Suspension bridges use long cables suspended from tall towers, called **pylons**, to hold the road, or deck, above the ground. The force of the deck, pushing down is matched by the **tension** in the cables and the **compression** in the pylons.

How a suspension bridge works

compression

compression

tension

gravity

Tall towers

The Millau Viaduct in France is the tallest bridge in the world, with a height of 1,125 feet (343 m)—taller than the **Eiffel Tower**.

1,125 feet (343 m)

The length of the world's longest bridge is greater than the distance between New York City and Philadelphia.

Driving across the world's longest bridge at 37 miles (60 km) per hour, it would take a car **about 2 hours, 45 minutes to complete the journey**.

LONGEST BRIDGES

1. **Danyang-Kunshan Grand Bridge (China)—540,700 feet (164,800 m)**
2. Tianjin Grand Bridge (China)—373,000 feet (113,700 m)
3. **Weinan Weihe Grand Bridge (China)—261,588 feet (79,732 m)**
4. Bang Na Expressway (Thailand)—177,000 feet (54,000 m)
5. **Beijing Grand Bridge (China)—157,982 feet (48,153 m)**
6. Lake Pontchartrain Causeway (United States)—126,122 feet (38,442 m)
7. **Manchac Swamp Bridge (United States)—120,440 feet (36,710 m)**
8. Yangcun Bridge (China)—117,493 feet (35,812 m)
9. **Hangzhou Bay Bridge (China)—117,037 feet (35,673 m)**
10. Runyang Bridge (China)—116,995 feet (35,660 m)

Widest bridge

The world's widest bridge is the San Francisco-Oakland Bay Bridge in California. It is **258.2 feet** (78.7 m) wide which is more than 33 feet (10 m) wider than the wingspan of a **747-8 jumbo jet**.

224.7 feet (68.5 m)

THAT DOESN'T LOOK RIGHT!

Some buildings are deliberately designed to look different, while others developed problems when they were built. The buildings shown here lean more than any others, some intentionally, while others have faults.

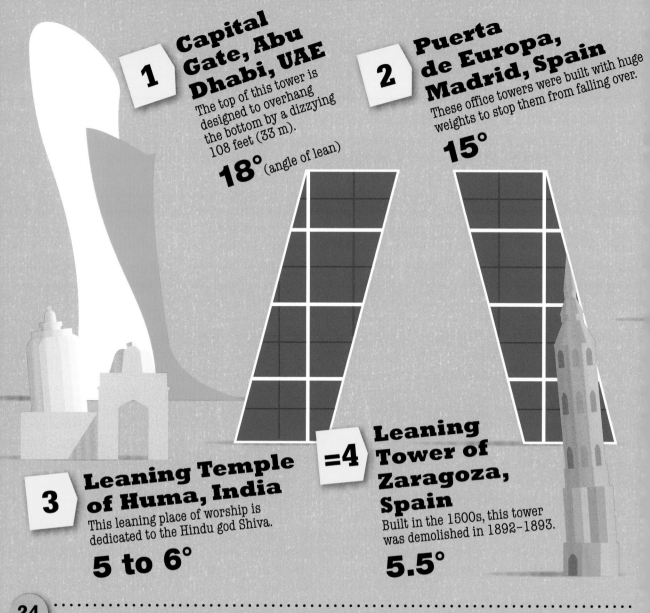

1 Capital Gate, Abu Dhabi, UAE
The top of this tower is designed to overhang the bottom by a dizzying 108 feet (33 m).
18° (angle of lean)

2 Puerta de Europa, Madrid, Spain
These office towers were built with huge weights to stop them from falling over.
15°

3 Leaning Temple of Huma, India
This leaning place of worship is dedicated to the Hindu god Shiva.
5 to 6°

=4 Leaning Tower of Zaragoza, Spain
Built in the 1500s, this tower was demolished in 1892–1893.
5.5°

Melting building

sunlight

Nicknamed the Walkie-Talkie, the curved shape of this building in London accidentally focuses sunlight on a spot in a nearby street. This creates temperatures of more than 194°F (90°C)—that's hot enough to melt plastic surfaces on cars and even to fry an egg!

=4 Leaning Tower of Niles, Illinois
Built in 1934, this is a half-sized replica of the Leaning Tower of Pisa.

5.5°

6 Leaning Tower of Suurhusen, Germany
The tower of this church started to lean when wooden beams rotted.

5.19°

7 Leaning Tower of Pisa
Built as a bell tower, this tower in Italy leans because it was built on soft ground and without an adequate foundation.

3.99°

8 Tower of Garisenda, Bologna, Italy
This is the shorter of two leaning towers in Bologna, but it leans more than the other.

3.8°

=9 Leaning Tower of Nevyansk, Russia
The lean on this tower was caused by the ground beneath subsiding.

3°

=9 Yunyan Pagoda, China
Cracks in supporting pillars have caused this 154-foot (47 m) tower to lean to one side.

3°

Before the Burj Khalifa, the tallest artificial structure was a radio mast built near Warsaw in Poland. It was 2,120.67 feet (646.38 m) tall—lying down, it would be as long as 45 buses. It collapsed on August 8, 1991.

SUPERDOMES

Because it has no sharp edges or flat surfaces, a dome is a very strong shape and can be used to cover a huge area. Domes are found on churches, markets, and stadiums.

Strong domes

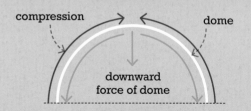

compression

dome

downward force of dome

Domes work in the same way as arches. Weight from the top of the dome is distributed down its walls, creating a pressure (or compression) that pushes the dome together, making it even stronger.

Saint Paul's Cathedral

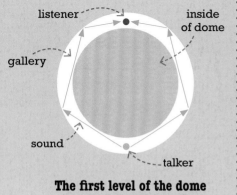

The dome of Saint Paul's, London, is one of the largest cathedral domes in the world. It weighs about **72,000 tons** (65,000 metric tons), which is about the same as a large aircraft carrier.

listener

inside of dome

gallery

sound

talker

The first level of the dome is called the Whispering Gallery. The special acoustics mean that a whisper made on one side of the gallery can be heard on the other.

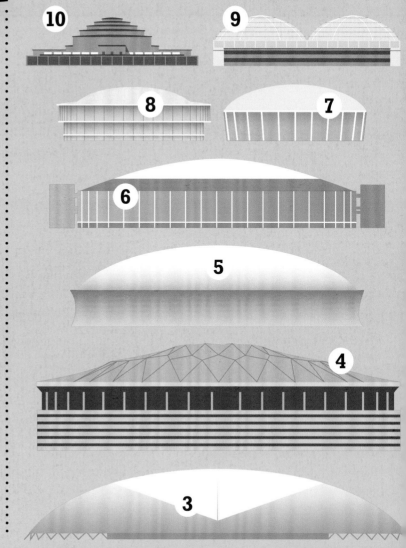

10

9

8

7

6

5

4

3

LARGEST DOMES THROUGH HISTORY (IN DIAMETER)

1. **Singapore National Stadium, Singapore (2014–)—1,024 feet (312 m)**

2. **Cowboys Stadium, United States (2009–2014)—902 feet (275 m)**

3. **Oita Stadium, Japan (2001–2009)—899 feet (274 m)**

4. **Georgia Dome, United States (1992–2001)—840 feet (256 m)**

5. **Louisiana Superdome, United States (1975–1992)—679 feet (207 m)**

6. **Astrodome, United States (1965–1975)—641.4 feet (195.5 m)**

7. **Belgrade Fair—Hall 1, Serbia (1957–1965)—358 feet (109 m)**

8. **Bojangles' Coliseum, United States (1955–1957)—333 feet (101.5 m)**

9. **Leipzig Market Hall, Germany (1930–1955)—214.9 feet (65.5 m)**

10. **Centennial Hall, Poland (1913–1930)—213 feet (65 m)**

2

1

The Singapore National Stadium is 270.7 feet (82.5 m) tall, which is about three-fifths the height of the Pyramid of Khufu (see page 19).

Geodesic domes

A geodesic dome combines arches and triangles to create a large but lightweight covering.

The Fukuoka Yafuoku! Dome, in Japan, is one of the largest geodesic domes in the world. This baseball stadium can seat **30,000 people**, and it is 276 feet (84 m) tall, almost as tall as the **Statue of Liberty**.

305 feet (93 m)

BUILDING IN SPACE

<····················>

Space stations are designed to support a human crew for many months. They are just like homes in space, with facilities for sleeping, eating, washing, and working.

1 **International Space Station (ISS)**
The ISS was built jointly by several countries.

32,030 cubic feet
(907 cu. m) (volume of pressurized space)

2 **Skylab (United States)**
This orbited Earth from 1973 until it re-entered and burned up in Earth's atmosphere in 1979.

12,710 cubic feet
(360 cu. m)

3 **Mir (USSR/ Russia)**
This was the first space station that was built in stages and it orbited from 1986 to 2001.

12,360 cubic

=6 Salyut 7 (USSR)

This was the last station that was part of the Salyut program and was replaced by Mir.

3,180 cubic feet (90 cu. m)

=6 Salyut 4 (USSR)

This space station made more than 12,000 orbits around Earth.

3,180 cubic feet (90 cu. m)

=6 Salyut 3 (USSR)

This space station was occupied for just 15 days.

3,180 cubic feet (90 cu. m)

=6 Salyut 6 (USSR)

This craft was the first space station to feature multiple docking ports.

3,180 cubic feet (90 cu. m)

10 Tiangong 1 (China)

China's first space station. Its name means "Heavenly Place."

508.5 cubic feet (14.4 cu. m)

ISS facts

The ISS weighs 462.37 tons (419.455 metric tons)—about the same as two blue whales.

It was built in stages— different modules were launched into space and put together in orbit. The first module, called Zarya, weighed just 21.3 tons (19.3 metric tons).

Zarya

The huge solar arrays can produce 110 kilowatts of total power, which is enough to power 55 homes.

It orbits at a speed of 17,400 miles (28,000 km) per hour, and it travels around about two-thirds of the planet every hour.

In a single day, it travels the equivalent distance from Earth to the moon and back.

The inside of the International Space Station has the same volume as a Boeing 747 jumbo jet—**enough to hold 19 million Ping-Pong balls!** It contains laboratories, an observatory, toilets and washing facilities, and living quarters for the astronauts.

GLOSSARY

accelerate
to increase speed

acoustics
the science of how sound waves behave as they travel through objects. This includes how sound travels through air.

acrylic
a type of plastic that is both lightweight and strong. Acrylic is a see-through plastic that is used to make the walls of large aquariums.

aquarium
a tank that is designed to hold water and aquatic animals, such as fish, crabs, and octopuses. The largest aquariums hold millions of gallons of water and hundreds of creatures.

barrow
an ancient burial mound

blimp
a type of airship without any form of rigid structure inside the envelope (the large bag used to hold the gas that lifts the craft into the air)

deck
on a bridge, the surface that carries traffic or pedestrians

geodesic dome
a type of dome that is made up of triangles

hectare
a unit used to measure land area. One hectare equals 2.5 acres.

inflation
when something increases in price

leasable area
the amount of space in a building that can be leased, or rented, for shops or offices

mall
a large building that contains lots of shops. Many malls offer other services, such as cinemas, theme parks, and restaurants to keep shoppers entertained.

module
a part or set of parts that can be joined with others to create a larger structure

pressurized space
in a space station, the part of the craft where the atmosphere is under pressure and breathable and where astronauts can survive without wearing a space suit

pylon
a tall vertical structure. On a suspension bridge, the pylons are the tall towers that support the long cables carrying the deck.

pyramid
a three-dimensional shape with triangular sides. Many civilizations built pyramid-shaped buildings to act as tombs or temples. For example, the ancient Egyptians built the Great Pyramids at Giza more than 4,500 years ago.

relic
the ancient remains of a saint or someone who was considered important

skyscraper
a tall building that has many floors and is used for offices, hotels, and apartments

solar array
the parts of a spacecraft that produce electricity from sunlight

space station
a type of spacecraft that is designed to orbit Earth and contain everything necessary to support a human crew

species
a group of organisms that share the same characteristics and are capable of breeding with one another to produce fertile offspring

suite
a group of rooms. A hotel suite can contain several rooms, including bedrooms, bathrooms, dining areas, a lounge, and a living room.

suspension bridge
a type of bridge that uses long cables hanging from towers to carry a deck that is suspended above the ground

tumulus
a large mound of earth and rock that has been built over a grave. The word is Latin for "small hill."

USSR
short for the Union of Soviet Socialist Republics. This was the name of the Communist nation of Russia and fourteen other republics.

WEBSITES

Cool Infographics
http://www.coolinfographics.com
This collection of infographics and data visualizations is from other online resources, magazines, and newspapers.

Daily Infographics
http://www.dailyinfographic.com
This comprehensive collection of infographics on an enormous range of topics is updated every day!

Data Visualization Encyclopedia
http://www.visualinformation.info
The website contains a whole host of infographic material on subjects as diverse as natural history, science, sports, and computer games.

Emporis
http://www.emporis.com
The website has facts, figures, information, and images about more than 400,000 important buildings around the world, including the tallest on the planet.

Guiness World Records
http://www.guinnessworldrecords.com
The website is for all things regarding record-breaking. It is packed with thousands of world records and facts.

NASA International Space Station
http://www.nasa.gov/mission_pages/station
The NASA website contains data, images, and records about the International Space Station.

INDEX

airports, **20–21**
Antilia, **9**
aquariums, **14–15**

bridges, **22–23**
British Museum, **10**
Burj al Arab, **9**
busiest airports, **21**

domes, **26–27**
Dubai Mall, **6**
Dubai Mall Aquarium, **15**

Eiffel Tower, **4**, **23**
Empire State Building, **5**, **16**

fastest roller coasters, **12–13**
Ferrari World, **13**
Forbidden City, **16–17**
Fukuoka Yafuoku! Dome, **27**

geodesic domes, **27**
Golden Gate Bridge, **22**
Grand Central Terminal, **21**

Hengqin Ocean Kingdom, **14–15**
Hotel President Wilson, **9**

International Space Station, **28–29**

Jungle Jim's, **7**

King Kullen, **7**
KL Bird Park, **14**

largest aquariums, **15**
largest domes, **27**
largest royal palaces, **17**
largest shopping malls, **7**
largest space stations, **28–29**

leaning buildings, **24–25**
longest bridges, **23**
Louvre, **11**, **16–17**

Marina Bay Sands, **8–9**
Millau Viaduct, **23**
most expensive buildings, **8–9**
most popular museums, **11**
museums, **10–11**

Palace of Parliament, **16–17**
palaces, **16–17**
ports, **20–21**

Saint Paul's Cathedral, **26**
San Francisco-Oakland Bay Bridge, **23**
Shanghai, **20–21**

Singapore National Stadium, **27**
Sistine Chapel, **11**
skyscrapers, **4–5**
Smithsonian Institution, **10**
space stations, **28–29**
suspension bridges, **22**

theme parks, **12–13**
Toronto Zoo, **15**
train stations, **21**

Versailles, Palace of, **16–17**

Walkie-Talkie building, **25**

zoos, **14–15**

First American edition published in 2016 by Lerner Publishing Group, Inc.
First published in 2015 by Wayland

Copyright © 2016 by Wayland
published by arrangement with Wayland

Hungry Tomato™ is a trademark of Lerner Publishing Group, Inc.

Hungry Tomato™
A division of Lerner Publishing Group, Inc.
241 First Avenue North
Minneapolis, MN 55401 USA

For reading levels and more information, look up this title at www.lernerbooks.com.

Main body text set in Rockwell Std. Typeface provided by Monotype.

Library of Congress Cataloging-in-Publication Data

Richards, Jon, 1970– author.
  Record-breaking building feats / by Jon Richards and Ed Simkins.
        pages cm. — (Infographic top 10s)
  Audience: Ages 9–12
  Audience: Grades 4 to 6
  Includes index.
  ISBN 978-1-4677-8594-5 (lb : alk. paper)
  ISBN 978-1-4677-9380-3 (pb : alk. paper)
  ISBN 978-1-4677-8645-4 (eb pdf)
  1. Buildings—Miscellanea—Juvenile literature.
2. Architecture—Miscellanea—Juvenile literature. I. Simkins, Ed, author. II. Title.
  TH149.R53 2016
  720.2—dc23   2015002515

Manufactured in the United States of America
1 – BP - 7/15/15